INKWELL

INSIGHTS

A Treasury of Creative Writing Sparks

Inkwell Insights by Kyra Schaefer
Copyright 2024 As You Wish Publishing
ISBN: 978-1-951131-63-0

Non-Fiction: Explore the impact of a personal challenge you've overcome, focusing on the lessons learned and personal growth.

Fiction: In a world where technology controls emotions, write a story about a character rebelling against a society that suppresses feelings.

Non-Fiction: Reflect on a moment in your life when you faced a difficult decision and how it shaped your future.

_____
_____
_____
_____
_____
_____
_____
_____
_____
_____
_____
_____
_____
_____
_____
_____
_____
_____
_____
_____
_____
_____
_____
_____
_____

Fiction: Create a story set in a future where AI companions are assigned to every person at birth, exploring the dynamics of human-robot relationships.

Non-Fiction: Share a personal travel experience that had a profound impact on your perspective and worldview.

Fiction: Write a mystery involving a detective who uses unconventional methods, such as interpreting dreams, to solve crimes.

Non-Fiction: Explore the importance of a specific cultural tradition in your life and how it has shaped your identity.

Fiction: In a dystopian society where books are banned, tell the story of an underground library that fights against censorship.

Non-Fiction: Reflect on a moment of failure in your life and the valuable lessons you gained from it.

Fiction: Create a story about a character who discovers they have the ability to enter paintings and interact with the depicted world.

Non-Fiction: Share the story of a person who inspired you and the impact they had on your life.

Fiction: Write about a group of friends who stumble upon a hidden cave with time-traveling abilities.

Non-Fiction: Reflect on the role of nature in your life and how it has influenced your well-being.

Fiction: In a world where dreams are shared collectively, explore the consequences when one person's nightmares affect the entire society.

Non-Fiction: Share a childhood memory that continues to shape your values and beliefs.

Fiction: Create a story about a person who can communicate with extraterrestrial beings through their dreams.

Non-Fiction: Reflect on a moment of unexpected kindness from a stranger that left a lasting impact on you.

Fiction: Write about a scientist who discovers a way to harness energy from dreams, leading to unforeseen consequences.

Non-Fiction: Explore a personal passion and how it has become a significant part of your life.

Fiction: In a society where memories can be bought and sold, tell the story of a person who discovers a black market for stolen memories.

Non-Fiction: Share the experience of a cultural celebration or festival that left a lasting impression on you.

Fiction: Create a story set in a world where people's reflections in mirrors have a life of their own.

Non-Fiction: Reflect on a time when you faced a fear and how overcoming it changed your perspective.

Fiction: Write about a person who can perceive emotions through colors and uses this ability to navigate social interactions.

Non-Fiction: Explore the impact of a specific book or piece of literature that has shaped your worldview.

Fiction: In a society where individuals can trade physical characteristics, tell the story of someone who discovers the consequences of such exchanges.

Non-Fiction: Share a personal experience that challenged your beliefs and led to personal growth.

Fiction: Create a story about a person who can manipulate probability, causing unexpected events in their life.

Non-Fiction: Reflect on a moment of resilience in the face of adversity and how it shaped your character.

_____

_____

_____

_____

_____

_____

_____

_____

_____

_____

_____

_____

_____

_____

_____

_____

_____

_____

_____

_____

_____

_____

_____

Fiction: In a future where people can access past lives through memories, explore the consequences of a person remembering a traumatic past.

Non-Fiction: Share the story of a mentor or role model who played a significant role in your life.

Fiction: Write about a character who discovers a hidden language that allows them to communicate with animals.

Non-Fiction: Reflect on a personal achievement that required perseverance and determination.

Fiction: Create a story about a town where every resident has a unique and uncontrollable supernatural talent.

Non-Fiction: Explore the impact of a specific historical event on your family or community.

_____

_____

_____

_____

_____

_____

_____

_____

_____

_____

_____

_____

_____

_____

_____

_____

_____

_____

_____

_____

_____

_____

_____

_____

_____

Fiction: In a society where individuals can switch bodies at will, tell the story of a person navigating the challenges of changing identities.

Non-Fiction: Share a moment of cultural exchange or cross-cultural friendship that broadened your perspective.

Fiction: Write about a person who can enter the dreams of others to explore and influence their subconscious.

Non-Fiction: Reflect on a personal goal you achieved against all odds, emphasizing the lessons learned during the journey.

Fiction: Create a story about a group of adventurers on a quest to find a mythical tree that holds the secret to immortality.

Non-Fiction: Share a moment when you had to make a difficult ethical decision and the impact it had on your life.

Fiction: In a world where emotions are personified entities, write about a person who befriends their own emotions.

Non-Fiction: Reflect on a period of personal transformation in your life and the factors that contributed to it.

Fiction: Write a mystery involving a character who can see auras, using this ability to solve crimes.

Non-Fiction: Share a personal story that highlights the importance of gratitude in your life.

Fiction: Create a story about a person who discovers a hidden doorway to a parallel universe in their own home.

Non-Fiction: Reflect on a moment of forgiveness in your life and how it impacted your relationships.

Fiction: In a future where people can manipulate weather, tell the story of a person with the power to control storms.

Non-Fiction: Explore the impact of a significant historical figure on your values and beliefs.

_____

_____

_____

_____

_____

_____

_____

_____

_____

_____

_____

_____

_____

_____

_____

_____

_____

_____

_____

_____

_____

_____

_____

_____

_____

Fiction: Write about a character who can manipulate sound waves, creating music with mystical effects.

Non-Fiction: Share a personal experience that challenged your cultural assumptions and led to greater understanding.

Fiction: Create a story about a person who can communicate with the consciousness of inanimate objects.

Non-Fiction: Reflect on a moment when you had to step out of your comfort zone and the positive outcomes that resulted.

Fiction: In a society where people can erase undesirable memories, explore the consequences of selective memory editing.

Non-Fiction: Share a moment when you had to confront a personal fear, exploring the emotions and growth that followed.

Fiction: Create a story about a group of friends who stumble upon a hidden underwater city with advanced technology.

Non-Fiction: Share the story of a personal passion
project that brought fulfillment and meaning to your life.

Fiction: In a world where people can enter paintings, tell the story of a person who becomes trapped in a masterpiece.

Non-Fiction: Explore the impact of a specific piece of art or music on your emotions and memories.

Fiction: Write about a person who discovers a hidden language that allows them to manipulate reality.

Non-Fiction: Reflect on a moment when you faced
imposter syndrome and how you overcame it.

Fiction: Create a story about a person who possesses the ability to understand and speak every language, including those of mythical creatures.

Non-Fiction: Share a moment when you had to navigate a cultural misunderstanding and the lessons learned.

Fiction: In a society where lies manifest as physical scars, explore the life of a brutally honest individual.

Non-Fiction: Reflect on a moment when you experienced a significant cultural celebration or ceremony.

Fiction: Write about a character who can manipulate shadows, creating illusions and controlling darkness.

Non-Fiction: Share the story of a personal setback and the resilience that helped you overcome it.

Fiction: In a future where dreams can be traded as a form of currency, explore the consequences of dream transactions.

Non-Fiction: Reflect on a moment when you had to confront a personal bias and the impact it had on your worldview.

Fiction: Create a story about a person who discovers a magical typewriter that allows them to rewrite moments of their past.

Non-Fiction: Share the story of a transformative journey, whether physical or metaphorical.

Fiction: Write about a group of explorers who discover a portal to a dimension where magic is real.

Non-Fiction: Reflect on a time when you had to navigate a cross-cultural friendship and the mutual understanding that developed.

Fiction: In a society where emotions are regulated by a governing body, tell the story of a person who rebels against emotional control.

Non-Fiction: Share a personal experience that challenged your beliefs about success and failure.

Fiction: Create a story about a character who can manipulate plant life, causing flowers to bloom or wither at will.

Non-Fiction: Reflect on a moment when you had to confront a personal prejudice and the changes it prompted.

Fiction: In a world where people age backward, explore the challenges and opportunities this presents for individuals and society.

Non-Fiction: Share the story of a personal achievement that required collaboration and teamwork.

Fiction: Write about a person who can travel between dimensions but struggles to find their way back home.

Non-Fiction: Reflect on a time when you had to navigate a cultural clash and the insights gained from the experience.

Fiction: Create a story about a person who discovers a forgotten language that has the power to reshape reality.

Non-Fiction: Share the impact of a specific historical event on your family's narrative.

Fiction: In a world where people can customize their personalities, tell the story of a person grappling with the authenticity of their identity.

Non-Fiction: Reflect on a moment when you had to confront your own biases and the steps you took to overcome them.

Fiction: Write about a person who can hear the thoughts of inanimate objects, exploring the challenges and humor that arise.

Non-Fiction: Share a personal experience that deepened your understanding of a different cultural perspective.

Fiction: In a future where people can upload their consciousness into virtual realities, explore the concept of digital immortality.

Non-Fiction: Reflect on a moment when you had to make a difficult ethical decision in your professional life.

Fiction: Create a story about a character who discovers a hidden society living beneath the Earth's surface.

Non-Fiction: Share a personal experience that highlighted the importance of empathy in your life.

Fiction: Write about a person who can enter mirrors and explore parallel reflections of reality.

Non-Fiction: Reflect on a moment when you had to navigate a workplace challenge and the skills you developed in the process.

Fiction: In a society where people can trade years of their lives for special abilities, explore the consequences of such transactions.

Non-Fiction: Share the story of a personal triumph over self-doubt and the strategies you employed for personal growth.

Fiction: Create a story about a person who can perceive time backward but struggles to live in the present.

Non-Fiction: Reflect on a moment when you faced a decision between conformity and authenticity.

Fiction: In a world where people can merge their consciousness with machines, tell the story of a person grappling with the loss of their humanity.

🌟 Unlock Your Writing Potential with As You Wish Publishing! 🌟

Are you an aspiring author with a story to share? As You Wish Publishing invites you to join our self-help collaboration books and embark on a journey to becoming a published author!

✨ Why Choose As You Wish Publishing?

- Collaborative Magic: We believe in the power of collective creativity! Our collaborative approach makes publishing accessible to first-time authors, fostering a supportive community.
- Guided Assistance: Fear not if you're new to the world of publishing! Our expert team provides step-by-step guidance, ensuring a smooth and enjoyable experience for writers of all levels.
- Diverse Voices: Embrace the richness of diverse perspectives. Join a vibrant community of writers who share their unique stories, creating books that resonate with a wide range of readers.
- Professional Quality: Your story deserves to shine! As You Wish Publishing maintains high standards of quality, delivering professionally produced books that you can proudly share with the world.

🎉 Join As You Wish Publishing Today!

Ready to make your mark in the world of publishing? Don't miss this opportunity to become a published author with As You Wish Publishing. Embrace collaboration, unlock your writing potential, and share your story with the world!

📧 email us at connect@asyouwishpublishing.com to start your publishing journey today.

🌐 Visit us at www.asyouwishpublishing.com for more information and to submit your story.

Made in United States
Troutdale, OR
07/26/2024

21538899R00111